BE A MAKER!

Maker Projects for Kids Who Love

PHOTOGRAPHY

KELLY SPENCE

Crabtree Publishing Company
www.crabtreebooks.com

Crabtree Publishing Company

www.crabtreebooks.com

Author: Kelly Spence

Series Research and Development: Reagan Miller

Editors: Sarah Eason, Harriet McGregor,
    Tim Cooke, and Philip Gebhardt

Proofreaders: Claudia Martin, Wendy Scavuzzo,
    and Petrice Custance

Editorial director: Kathy Middleton

Design: Paul Myerscough

Cover design: Paul Myerscough

Photo research: Rachel Blount

**Production coordinator and
    Prepress technician:** Tammy McGarr

Print coordinator: Katherine Berti

Consultant: Jennifer Turliuk, Bachelor of Commerce,
Singularity University Graduate Studies Program at
NASA Ames, Former President of MakerKids

Production coordinated by Calcium Creative

Photo Credits:

t=Top, bl=Bottom Left, br=Bottom Right

Ollie Baker: www.frankencamera.wordpress.com: p. 7; Panomo: p. 27;
Shutterstock: Blend Images: p. 5; Maria Gaellman: p. 4; Gorillaimages:
p. 6; Iakov Kalinin: pp. 19, 29b; Krunja: p. 14; NoPainNoGain: p. 10;
NorGal: pp. 1, 18; Fesus Robert: p. 16; Yuriy Rudyy: p. 11; Scanrail1:
p. 22; E. Spek: p. 23; Stocked House Studio: p. 9; Tulpahn: p. 24; Chamille
White: p. 26; Zoom Team: p. 25; Tudor Photography: pp. 12–13, 20–21,
28–29; Wikimedia Commons: p. 8; Aljawad: p. 15; Robert Scoble: p. 17.

Cover: Tudor Photography

Library and Archives Canada Cataloguing in Publication

Spence, Kelly, author
    Maker projects for kids who love photography /
Kelly Spence.

(Be a maker!)
Includes index.
Issued in print and electronic formats.
ISBN 978-0-7787-2578-7 (hardback).--
ISBN 978-0-7787-2584-8 (paperback).--
ISBN 978-1-4271-1766-3 (html)

    1. Photography--Juvenile literature. 2. Cameras--Juvenile
literature. I. Title.

TR149 S74 2016   j770   C2016-903334-1
                                          C2016-903335-X

Library of Congress Cataloging-in-Publication Data

Names: Spence, Kelly, author.
Title: Maker projects for kids who love photography / Kelly
Spence.
Description: St. Catharines, Ontario ; New York, New York :
Crabtree Publishing Company, [2016] | Series: Be a maker! |
Includes index.
Identifiers: LCCN 2016026032 (print) | LCCN 2016026735 (ebook)
ISBN 9780778725787 (reinforced library binding) |
ISBN 9780778725848 (pbk.) |
ISBN 9781427117663 (Electronic HTML)
Subjects: LCSH: Photography--Juvenile literature. |
Cameras--Juvenile literature. | Makerspaces--Juvenile literature.
Classification: LCC TR149 .S634 2016 (print) |
LCC TR149 (ebook) | DDC 770--dc23
LC record available at https://lccn.loc.gov/2016026032

Crabtree Publishing Company

www.crabtreebooks.com   1-800-387-7650

Printed in Canada/072016/EF20160630

Published in Canada
Crabtree Publishing
616 Welland Ave.
St. Catharines, Ontario
L2M 5V6

Published in the United States
Crabtree Publishing
PMB 59051
350 Fifth Avenue, 59th Floor
New York, New York 10118

Published in the United Kingdom
Crabtree Publishing
Maritime House
Basin Road North, Hove
BN41 1WR

Published in Australia
Crabtree Publishing
3 Charles Street
Coburg North
VIC, 3058

CONTENTS

Say Cheese!	4
Beyond Words	6
History of Photography	8
Look, Snap, See	10
Make It! A Pinhole Viewer	12
Going Digital	14
Different Shots	16
Gear Guide	18
Make It! A Light Tent	20
Editing Your Work	22
Creative Connections	24
New Directions	26
Make It! Green Screen Photography	28
Glossary	30
Learning More	31
Index	32

SAY CHEESE!

American photographer Ansel Adams once said: "You don't take a photograph—you make it!" A photograph can be more than just a record. It can also be art. By looking at a subject in new ways, and controlling the elements that make a great shot, a photographer can make a photo express ideas and emotions.

CREATING PHOTOGRAPHS

People have been fascinated by light for thousands of years. The first photographs were created by combining **optics**, or the science of light, with chemical reactions. Digital photography pairs optics with technology to produce electronic images. Today, technology has advanced so far that, within a few minutes, anyone can snap a photo, edit it, and share it with countless others.

THE MAKER MOVEMENT

What exactly is a maker? A maker is anyone who builds or creates something. But there is more to the maker movement than just creating. Makers ask questions. They think "outside the box," and ask, "What if?" They know that there are often several ways to approach any project. Making is about **innovation**, or putting a new twist on something that already exists.

Capturing an action shot is all about timing. Snapping multiple pictures in a row provides lots of images to choose from.

READY, SET, MAKE!

Makers come together in **makerspaces**. Many schools, libraries, and museums house makerspaces designed to inspire, educate, and innovate. However, if you have a camera, smartphone, or tablet, a makerspace can be anywhere. Makerspaces provide a place to share your ideas and ask questions about other people's projects. There are also online communities that connect makers from around the world. Make sure you ask a responsible adult to check any websites you use.

START NOW!

Anyone can be a shutterbug. Some photographers pair their interest in art and technology with their favorite pastimes. If you are a sports fan, try capturing action on the field. If you like writing, snap some shots to showcase alongside your stories or poems. The best way to learn about photography and to get your creative juices flowing is to start snapping pictures. So, grab your camera, smartphone, or tablet, and get started!

Teamwork is key to the maker movement. Makers get new ideas by **collaborating**, or working with others. Use your imagination and have fun!

BEYOND WORDS

Images can be incredibly powerful. They can be used to record a special person, place, or event. From family snapshots to advertisements, photographs are all around us. Before the camera was invented, people captured images by painting and drawing. Creative makers are using technology to change the way people experience art.

MORE THAN WORDS

Photographs can evoke, or bring out, powerful emotions. Images are universal, so they can be experienced by anyone, no matter what language they speak or what country they live in. In **photojournalism**, still images can convey or capture an emotion or statement that is impossible to express in words.

OPTICAL ILLUSIONS

Seeing is not always believing. Using **point of view**, **scale**, and other techniques to trick the viewer's eye are fun ways to use a camera. Some of these trick pictures have become popular at tourist attractions, such as the Leaning Tower of Pisa in Italy. Tourists often pose near the tower, which tips to one side. They position themselves so they appear to be holding the tower up.

To set up this trick shot, the girl is positioned to look as though she is holding the tower up. Other tourists pose to look as though they are pushing the tower over. How would you set up your shot?

EXPOSED!

A picture's **exposure** is determined by the amount of light the camera captures, and for how long it enters the camera. This is controlled by the camera's **aperture**, **shutter speed**, and **ISO**. If too much light is used, parts of the photograph will appear overexposed, or washed-out. If there is not enough light, the shot will appear underexposed, or dark. Many digital cameras adjust automatically, depending on the light they detect. However, you can get creative and override the camera's settings to try out different exposures in your work.

NEAR AND FAR

Every photograph has a **depth of field**. This is how much of the picture appears in focus. If a photographer wants to draw the viewer's eye to something in the front of the picture, they use a shallow depth of field. This is achieved by shooting a **subject** close up and allowing more light into the camera. The subject appears sharp, while the background is blurry. A deeper depth of field shows more of the image in focus, and allows less light into the camera.

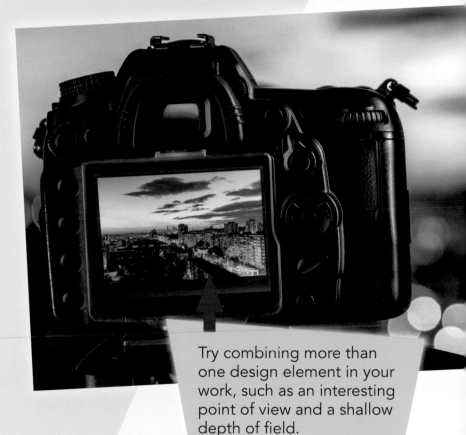

Try combining more than one design element in your work, such as an interesting point of view and a shallow depth of field.

Be a Maker!

Look at the world around you, and brainstorm how you can use point of view in your pictures. What happens if you change the angle you are shooting from? Can you make something appear much larger or smaller? Experiment with placing your subject closer to and farther away from the camera. Use your imagination!

HISTORY OF PHOTOGRAPHY

The word "photography" comes from the Greek words *photos*, meaning "light," and *graphos*, meaning "writing." Since ancient times, people have been fascinated by light.

EYE SPY

Light travels in straight lines. A camera obscura consists of a dark box with a small hole in one end. When reflected light enters through the opening, it forms an upside-down picture. These early devices were used by artists to trace pictures.

This image shows how a camera obscura works.

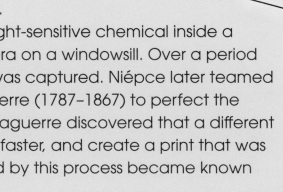

PERMANENT PICTURES

In 1826, the **lithographer** and inventor Joseph Nicéphore Niépce created the world's first photograph. He placed a plate covered with a light-sensitive chemical inside a camera obscura, then set the camera on a windowsill. Over a period of eight hours, the first photograph was captured. Niépce later teamed up with Louis-Jacques-Mandé Daguerre (1787–1867) to perfect the photo-making process. Over time, Daguerre discovered that a different chemical could develop the image faster, and create a print that was much sharper. The images produced by this process became known as daguerreotypes.

KODAK MOMENTS

In 1888, American George Eastman (1854–1932) was invited on a photography trip with a friend. He gathered all the equipment he needed, although he did not make the trip in the end. Eastman decided to make taking pictures so easy that anyone could become a photographer. In 1900, his company Kodak, introduced the $1 Brownie camera. Once a roll of film was shot, people mailed the camera to Kodak, where the pictures were developed and the film was replaced.

SHAKE IT LIKE A POLAROID

What is even better than flexible film? Instant pictures! In 1948, the Polaroid camera was launched as the world's first instant camera. It allowed users to snap a picture, and watch it magically appear in less than a minute.

Film packets treated with chemicals are loaded directly into a Polaroid camera. They develop an image seconds after a picture is taken.

Be a Maker!

Early makers learned how to capture images using their knowledge of scientific principles and mechanics. But a passion for pictures and a clear understanding of how light works were important stepping stones to better pictures. George Eastman said: "Light makes photography. Embrace light. Admire it. Love it. But above all, know light. Know it for all you are worth, and you will know the key to photography." What do you know about light? How might thinking about light shape your approach to photography?

LOOK, SNAP, SEE

All cameras work using the same basic technology. Understanding how light is captured and focused by the different parts of a camera is helpful for setting up your shots.

CAPTURING LIGHT

The light is collected and focused by a **lens** made of a curved, clear material such as glass or plastic. This is also how the human eye receives images. The image is upside-down. While the brain automatically flips an image, a camera uses a mirror to correct it. A photographer presses a button to activate the camera's **shutter**. The shutter acts like a pair of curtains drawn across the sensor. The width of the gap between the two curtains determines how long light is allowed to fall on the sensor. The aperture is like a window. The size of the aperture controls the amount of light that enters the camera. The shutter speed controls how long the shutter is open. Together, the aperture and shutter speed determine a picture's exposure.

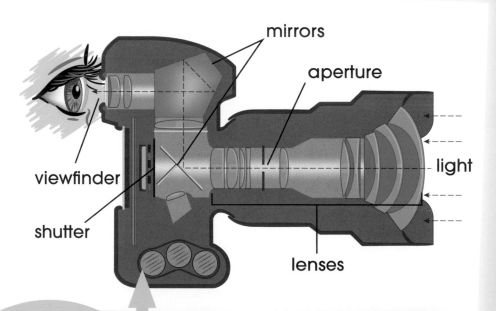

mirrors

aperture

viewfinder

light

shutter

lenses

A digital camera uses mirrors and lenses to capture light and convert it into an image that is displayed on an electronic screen.

FOCUS!

Think about what is important in your photo. The depth of field is how much of a picture appears in focus. A large aperture is good for close-up shots because it creates a shallow depth of field. A small aperture creates a greater depth of field. Aperture is measured in f-stops. The lower the number of the f-stop, the larger the aperture.

On some lenses, the f-stop numbers are divided in half (or by 2) each time. On these lenses, as the f-stop numbers decrease by half, the amount of light the lens lets in doubles. For example, an f-stop of f/2.8 halved is f/1.4, so f/1.4 lets in double the amount of light of f/2.8. The best way to learn about f-stops is to practice. To start, set several objects at different distances from the camera. Take multiple shots using the different f-stops on your camera. Which f-stop best captures the focus of your shot? How do the depths of field change the image?

FROM NEGATIVE TO POSITIVE

In a film camera, light strikes the film, which is coated with chemicals. The incoming light reacts with the chemicals, which store the reflected light from whatever is being photographed. The film must be kept in a dark, sealed container. If it is exposed to light, the images will be lost. The film is developed in a **darkroom**, where it is dipped into several chemicals. The chemicals produce a **negative** image on the film. On the negative, areas that were bright appear dark, and areas that were dark appear bright.

When you hold a strip of negatives up to the light, you see a reverse image in which light areas appear dark, and dark areas appear light.

MAKE IT!
A PINHOLE VIEWER

Before getting started with a high-tech digital camera, build your very own pinhole viewer! See for yourself how light is focused through an aperture and captured to project an image inside a camera.

YOU WILL NEED
- Narrow cardboard tube with solid bottom
- Black construction paper
- Translucent paper
- Elastic band
- Glue
- Aluminum foil
- Marker
- Push pin
- Craft knife
- Tape

1
- Wipe clean the inside of the tube. Use a piece of black construction paper to line the inside of the tube.
- With a marker, draw a line around the tube, about 2 inches (5 cm) from the bottom (the solid end) of the tube. Ask an adult to help you cut along the line so that you have two pieces.
- Using a push pin, punch a hole in the center of the bottom of the short tube.

2
- Cover the open end of the short tube with translucent, or tracing paper. Use an elastic band to hold it in position. The paper will be your screen.
- Put the longer piece of tube on top of the shorter piece. Make sure the hole at the bottom of the short tube is facing outward. Tape the pieces together.

3 To keep light out, wrap a piece of foil twice around the whole tube. Tuck the loose ends into the open top of the tube. Shape the ends at the bottom of the tube around the edge. Tape the edges.

4 Close one eye. Cup your hands around the open end of the tube, and hold it to your other eye. It needs to be as dark as possible inside the tube. Point the tube toward any object. The translucent paper makes a screen that shows an upside-down color image of the object. The image is created by light entering through the pinhole in the end of the tube.

Make It Even Better!

See what happens when you make the hole larger. Try inserting a lens into the hole. You might try a lens from an old pair of eyeglasses. How does the image change?

CONCLUSION

Take a look at your finished pinhole viewer. Check if there are any spots that need to be covered better. Would a different material be better at blocking out light? Or would a different-shaped container work better?

GOING DIGITAL

Makers are always challenging themselves. They love to try out new technology. Cameras are always changing.

FAREWELL, FILM!

A digital camera collects light through a shutter and lens, just like a film camera. But instead of using chemicals and film, the light is turned into electrical signals. These signals become a digital image made up of tiny squares of color called **pixels**. The more pixels a photo has in a given area, the higher the **resolution**. The picture appears on a **liquid-crystal-display** (LCD) screen. The photo can be deleted or stored in the camera.

BAD BUSINESS

The first digital camera was invented at Kodak in 1975. But the company did not want to lose business from developing film into prints, so the technology was shelved. By 1989, engineers had improved the design. They created the first digital single-lens reflex (DSLR) camera. But Kodak was still making money from film. Instead of building digital cameras, they sold licenses that allowed other companies to use the technology. This proved bad for business. Digital photography has exploded, but Kodak has struggled to keep up with its competitors—even though they got their start using Kodak's original technology!

When a low-resolution picture is blown up, you can see the individual square pixels. With a higher resolution, the image would appear sharper.

Makers and Shakers

Steve Sasson

American Steve Sasson (born 1950) is a maker who was ahead of his time. He invented the digital camera at age 24, while working as an engineer for Kodak. Sasson's first digital camera weighed a hefty 8 pounds (3.6 kg). He built it using parts from other cameras. This first model took 23 seconds to record a black-and-white image on a cassette tape. Today, that camera is on display at the National Museum of American History in Washington, D.C.

In 2011, Sasson was inducted into the National Inventors Hall of Fame for developing the first digital camera.

CAMERA IN YOUR POCKET

Since the late 2000s, mobile photography has made it easier than ever to capture amazing pictures. Most smartphones and tablets include a built-in camera. Some phones and tablets have two cameras. These devices pack a lot of power into a small package. Cell phone cameras can capture millions of pixels in each frame. Once you have made the perfect shot, you can edit, enhance, or share your pictures with a few taps of your finger. Explore the different settings and apps available for your device and try out different effects on your favorite pics.

DIFFERENT SHOTS

Photography makers combine technology and creativity to capture all sorts of pictures. Whether you are using film or a digital camera, there are different elements to think about when you put together a photo.

PARTS OF A PICTURE

The subject is the focus of your shot. The background is everything that falls behind the subject, and the foreground is anything in front. The photo's **composition** is how these elements work together.

MASTERING MODES

Most digital cameras have different **modes** for snapping specific kinds of pictures.

Portraits: In portrait mode, using a larger aperture creates a blurred background. This keeps the focus on the subject.

Macro Shots: Macro, or close-up, shots make tiny subjects appear larger. These images have a shallow depth of field, so the camera must be held steady.

Action Shots: For action shots, a quick shutter captures subjects on the move.

Landscapes: Using landscape mode, the camera's settings adjust to bring the entire frame into focus.

In this landscape, the horizon line falls across the bottom third of the frame. The bale of hay is positioned off-center where this line intersects with another. Think about how you can use the **rule of thirds** in your work.

Makers and Shakers

Annie Leibovitz

Famous for her portraits that use bold colors and **composite** backgrounds to tell a story, Annie Leibovitz (born 1949) has shot famous covers for *Rolling Stone* and *Vanity Fair*. She was the first woman to have her work displayed at the National Gallery in Washington, DC, and has been named a living legend by the Library of Congress. After more than four decades behind the lens, she continues to capture amazing pictures. According to Annie, a "photographer's eye" is never closed: "One doesn't stop seeing. One doesn't stop framing. It doesn't turn off and turn on. It's on all the time."

Annie Leibovitz first discovered a love for photography while studying painting at university.

THE RULE OF THIRDS

The rule of thirds subdivides a photograph to help the photographer compose the image. Imagine two vertical lines dividing the image from left to right into thirds. Now place two horizontal lines so they divide the image into thirds from top to bottom. Photographers often place interesting elements of the photograph along one or more of these lines. They place the most interesting feature at one of the four points where the lines intersect. Experienced photographers often break this rule, however. They sometimes put the subject in the middle of the photograph. Look through a magazine. Can you find photographs that use the rule of thirds? Try using the rule when taking a picture of someone.

GEAR GUIDE

Makers have created tons of extra gear that allows shutterbugs to capture a tricky shot or achieve a certain feel. Here is the lowdown on some of the hardware available today.

SOLID AND STEADY

A **tripod** is a three-legged stand used to support a camera. It holds a camera steady to keep images in focus. In college, maker JoeBen Bevirt was challenged to come up with an innovative design for a tripod. Bevirt's group designed a tripod with bendable legs—and the Gorillapod was born. The tripod is lightweight, portable, and can be wrapped around just about anything. In true maker fashion, Bevirt's company has dreamed up more new ideas that build on the original design. These include a Gorillapod that can hold a smartphone, and another with magnetic feet that stick to metal.

CONTROLLING LIGHT

Most cameras have a built-in flash that brightens up a dark shot. An additional flash can also be added to the camera to focus light on a specific spot. Other add-ons, such as a **diffuser**, spread the light from the flash. This tones down harsh light and creates softer shadows. A diffuser is often used in portraits.

With a flexible tripod such as the Gorillapod, you can capture images from almost any angle you shoot from.

LOOKING AT LENSES

Lenses and filters are attached to a camera to achieve different looks in your pictures. **Bokeh** (BOH-kay), meaning "blur" in Japanese, is a technique that creates an out-of-focus blur in a photo. It is achieved using a wide aperture. Filters are thin pieces of glass or plastic that are screwed onto the camera lens. Some filters are used to protect the lens, while others create special effects.

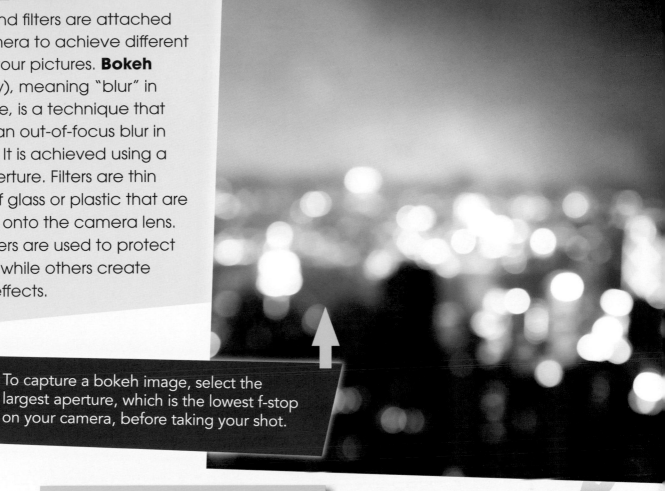

To capture a bokeh image, select the largest aperture, which is the lowest f-stop on your camera, before taking your shot.

Be a Maker!

Makers are always ready to improvise and try out new ideas. To reduce camera shake, you can use your body as a tripod. Stand with your legs shoulder width apart, hold the camera with two hands, and press your elbows together. Or, lean against a wall or tree to stabilize yourself before you snap your shot. Is there a solid surface you could set your camera on? Is there a different position that would work better for your shot, or offer a fresh perspective? What materials could you use to make your own tripod?

MAKE IT!
A LIGHT TENT

Photography gear does not need to be fancy or expensive. You can recycle some of your old binders to create your own portable light tent. This is a handy tool to have on hand when shooting macro shots. The translucent plastic of the binders diffuses light, creating a soft glow with few shadows. This will showcase the detail of your subject.

YOU WILL NEED
- 3 translucent ring binders
- Duct tape
- Colored card stock
- Paper clips
- A subject
- Digital camera

1
- Lay one binder flat and open. Lay a second binder over the top so that one of its flaps covers the flap of the lower binder.
- Use duct tape to join the binders where the edge of one binder meets the fold of the other.

2
- Attach a piece of colored card stock using paper clips to form a colored background.
- Cut the cover off the third binder. Tape the cover to the central panel at its top edge. It will be a roof.

3 ● Open your light tent into a cube, with the colored card hanging down at the back. If the roof is too loose, use tape to hold it in place.

● Place your subject inside the light tent.
● Try out different viewpoints to figure out which will work best when you start shooting. Decide if you need to adjust the background, too.

4

5 ● Start snapping pictures. Try shooting from different angles to show your subject from all sides. Keep your hands steady or use a tripod to reduce camera shake.

CONCLUSION

How effective was the light tent at removing shadows from your shots? What other materials could you use to diffuse light? Take your light tent outside to capture flowers and insects in their environment. How does your design work with light from different directions?

Make It Even Better!

Try using colored binders to see what color works best with your subject. Try using the manual and automatic macro settings on your camera. Which works better?

EDITING YOUR WORK

A photographer's creativity does not end with the click of the shutter. Once you have captured a digital image, there are countless ways to manipulate, or change, it. Photos can be altered and saved in different formats until you are happy with the finished product.

FILE FORMATS

A photograph can be saved in multiple formats. JPEGs, named for the Joint Photographic Experts Group, are the most common format to store photos in. These files work with most computers and software, and also do not take up a lot of storage space. A Tagged Image Format File (TIFF) is a larger file format. A RAW file captures the most detail, but requires a lot of computer memory. This format is most common among professional photographers.

TOOLS OF THE TRADE

There are several photo-editing programs and apps that let you edit, correct, and enhance your pictures. Some are built into a device such as a tablet or smartphone, while others must be installed on a computer. Free software is often available online, but check with an adult before downloading any programs. Try out some of the following cool techniques.

With photo-editing software, you can make a garden of tulips any color you like.

WHAT STAYS, WHAT GOES

Cropping is a tool that removes unwanted parts of a photo. Think about what you want to showcase, and whether it will stand out better if something else is removed. If you want to lighten a subject, or draw the viewer's eye to it, try using the **dodging** tool. Use the **burning** tool to darken parts of the image that appear too light.

FUN TOUCHES

It is best to capture your digital images in color. You can always edit your photos to try out effects such as black and white, sepia (pale brown), and **infrared**. If you are shooting with a camera phone, there are tons of cool apps that let users apply different effects to their shots. Filters allow you to add fun backgrounds, give the photo a vintage look, and much more. See what works best for your shots.

The right side of this photograph is shown in sepia, which makes the picture look old-fashioned. In contrast, the left side in full color brings the guinea pig to life.

Be a Maker!

Try different editing techniques on the same photo. Save them all, then compare the end results. What happens when you zoom in on a certain feature? Does changing the color enhance your work? Which techniques work best to share your message? Ask others for feedback. Mix it up. Swap pictures with some of your friends and see what techniques they try on your work.

CREATIVE CONNECTIONS

Making is all about sharing. At one time, the only way to share photos was to get together and flip through photo albums. Since the creation of the Internet, online photo sharing has boomed. Today, anyone can send and receive pictures from anywhere in the world with the click of a button.

A COMMUNITY OF MAKERS

There are entire communities of online makers who specialize in photography. These are great places to get feedback, learn new techniques, and find inspiration. Make sure to check with a parent or teacher before signing up for a photo-sharing community, and never post pictures that share personal information. Start your own photo blog to share your pictures with family and friends.

Maker faires are special events where makers meet and share their ideas. But you do not need to attend a faire to share your projects. Check to see if local libraries, museums, or restaurants feature local artists. Ask if you can display your work, or set up a showing for your family and friends.

PLAYING WITH PRINTS

While printed pictures are not as common today as they once were, you can still use your creativity to display your work in innovative ways. Create a photo book, a birthday card, or a photo cube with your pictures. Even older prints can be made new again by using a scanner to create a digital copy.

Instagram is a popular photo-sharing app and social network designed for smartphones. In the app, users can edit their pictures and apply different filters before sharing their work with family and friends.

Makers and Shakers

Zev Hoover

At just 14, maker Zev Hoover (born 1999) of Natick, Massachusetts, became an Internet sensation with his photographs of miniature people. He is known online as "Fiddleoak," a play on words of "little folk." Hoover has more than 70,000 followers on the popular photo-sharing site Flickr. He builds composite images of people that he shrinks down and places in natural settings. Hoover's work is a collaborative process. His older sister Aliza helps him come up with ideas, then Zev builds the pictures.

INSIDE A MAKER'S MIND

Zev Hoover shares his process with other photographers on his blog. Each picture he creates requires several steps. For one shot, he spent three hours taking shots of paper airplanes tied to strings. He then took pictures of himself hanging from a pole, and used Photoshop to combine the images. The finished shot seems to show a miniature Hoover piloting a paper airplane. You can use toys, close-ups, and different points of view to create your own "trick" photographs.

The photographer has made tiny sunbathers look life-size in this picture by playing with scale. What background materials could you use to create illusions?

NEW DIRECTIONS

Whether through hardware, techniques, or editing, photography makers are always looking for new ways to capture and share an image.

OLD MADE NEW

Photography equipment is often expensive. But you do not need fancy cameras and lenses to become a shutterbug. Think outside the box. Ask your family or friends if they have an old camera they are no longer using, or check out flea markets and yard sales for bargains. Some makers upcycle old camera parts such as a lens or flash to add to their digital cameras. Check out maker websites for inspiration, and be sure to share your own ideas, too. You never know what will inspire your next great shot!

SEEING GREEN

Today, green-screen technology is used in both photography and video production. This technique uses **chroma-key** technology to separate a subject from the background. Using an app or software program, the green background is keyed out, or removed.

Some photographers prefer using manual cameras instead of digital cameras. Experiment with both and see which type of camera best brings your pictures to life.

A photographer can then add in whatever background he or she chooses. This technique is popular for portraits. It is much easier—and cheaper—than creating a full backdrop in a studio.

OUT OF THIS WORLD!

From a tiny camera that fits on your finger to a room-sized camera obscura, makers are forever pushing the limits—even to the edge of our solar system! For decades, scientists have sent high-tech cameras to explore far-off planets. In 2012, the space robot Curiosity sent back its first selfie from the surface of Mars. In 2015, the first close-up shots of the dwarf planet Pluto were beamed back more than 3 billion miles (4.8 billion km) to scientists on Earth.

The Panono camera is about the size of a grapefruit and weighs a little more than 1 pound (2.2 kg).

Makers and Shakers

Jonas Pfeil

German maker Jonas Pfeil (born 1983) has taken digital photography outside of the box—or rather inside the ball. Pfeil invented a ball camera, called the Panono, with 36 cameras built into it. Each individual camera captures images at a very high resolution. When the ball is thrown into the air, a sensor sends a signal to the cameras to fire at its highest point. The cameras can also be controlled remotely by an app or by a button. The digital images are then joined to create a full **panoramic** image.

MAKE IT!
GREEN SCREEN PHOTOGRAPHY

With a green screen, you can put your subject anywhere. Team up with a friend to build your own green-screen studio. After taking your shot, swap out the green screen for a new background.

YOU WILL NEED
- Green fabric or paper
- Large board
- Duct tape
- Props
- Smartphone or digital camera
- A green screen app or photo-editing program

1 ● Cover your board with the green paper or fabric. Fold it over the edges of the board and stick it down on the back with duct tape.

2 ● Use the timer on your camera to take a picture of yourself in front of the screen. Use props that will fit in with the final image. Avoid standing too close to the screen, and avoid using lighting that creates strong shadows.

- Choose or take a picture for your background. You can find background images on the Internet. Make sure you have permission to use images from their original owner, or access collections through free stock photography websites.

3

4

- Using a green screen app or photo-editing program, combine the two pictures. What kinds of unusual locations can you put yourself in?

CONCLUSION

How effective was the green paper or fabric at creating a smooth backdrop? Would using a different material achieve a better-looking picture? What other props could you use to tell a story or get across your message?

Make It Even Better!

Try out different backgrounds and poses. Create a photo book by shooting images in sequence that tell a story. Use photo-editing tools to further enhance your finished product.

GLOSSARY

aperture The opening in a camera that controls the amount of light traveling through the lens

bokeh A composition technique, achieved with a lens, that leaves part of a photograph out of focus

burning A technique in which parts of a photograph are darkened

chroma-key An editing technique in which a specific color is blocked out in an image

collaborating Working together

composite Describing something that is made up of several elements

composition How the parts of a picture work together

darkroom A room without natural light, used for developing photographs

depth of field The zone or distance in which objects in front of or behind the subject are in focus

diffuser A device that spreads and evens out light

dodging A technique in which parts of a photograph are lightened

exposure The amount of light required to produce a photograph

infrared Light that is invisible to the human eye; In photography, it is captured by special film or sensors

innovation Introducing something new

ISO International Standards Organizatioin, a measure of how sensitive a camera's film or image sensor is to light

lens A clear, curved piece of glass or plastic that directs light

liquid-crystal-display An electric screen on which images are displayed

lithographer Someone who makes prints from a flat surface that has been prepared so ink only sticks to the design to be printed

makerspaces Places where makers come together to share ideas, innovate, and invent

modes Predetermined settings on a camera

panoramic Covering a wide view

photojournalism A medium that uses pictures to tell a news story

pixels The smallest parts of an image, measured in pixels per inch (ppi)

point of view Refers to the direction from which something is viewed

resolution The ability to show detail

rule of thirds A composition technique in which the subject is placed at specific vertical and horizontal points

scale The size an object appears to be in comparison to something else

shutter The part of a camera that opens and closes to let light enter

shutter speed How quickly a camera's shutter opens and closes

subject The main idea or object in a picture

tripod A three-legged stand used to stabilize a camera

LEARNING MORE

BOOKS

Bidner, Jenni. *The Kids' Guide to Digital Photography: How to Shoot, Save, Play with & Print Your Digital Photos*. Sterling, 2011.

Ebert, Michael, and Sandra Abend. *Photography for Kids! A Fun Guide to Digital Photography*. Rocky Nook Inc., 2011.

Gatcum, Chris. *The Beginner's Photography Guide*. DK Publishing, 2013.

Honovich, Nancy, and Annie Griffiths. *National Geographic Kids Guide to Photography: Tips & Tricks on How to Be a Great Photographer From the Pros & Your Pals at MyShot*. National Geographic Kids, 2015.

WEBSITES

Find out more about Zev Hoover and his little folk projects on his blog:
https://fiddleoak.wordpress.com

Visit the "Common Sense Media" website for a list of kid- and teen-friendly apps that allow users to apply different treatments to their pictures, and share their work online in a safe environment. Be sure to ask permission from an adult before downloading any apps to a device:
www.commonsensemedia.org/lists/photography-apps-for-kids-and-teens

Check out some of the cool photography projects available from "Make":
www.makezine.com/tag/photography

National Geographic's "MyShot" is a moderated platform for young shutterbugs to share their work. The site runs contests and offers tips for capturing unique shots and perspectives:
http://kids-myshot.nationalgeographic.com

INDEX

Adams, Ansel 4
aperture 7, 10, 12, 16, 19

Bevirt, JoeBen 18
bokeh 19
burning tool 23

camera obscura 8, 27
chroma-key technology 26, 27–29
collaboration 5, 25
composition 16, 17
cropping 23
Curiosity 27

Daguerre, Louis-Jacques-Mandé 8
depth of field 7, 10, 11, 16
digital photography 4, 7, 10, 14, 15, 16,
    22, 23, 27, 28
dodging tool 23

Eastman, George 9
editing photographs 4, 15, 22, 23, 24,
    26, 29
effects, special 15, 19, 23
equipment 9, 18, 19, 20, 26
exposure 7, 10, 11

f-stops 10, 11, 19
film 9, 11, 14, 16
filters 19, 23, 24

green-screen technology 26, 28–29

history of photography 8, 9
Hoover, Zev 25

Instagram 24

Kodak 9, 14, 15

Leibovitz, Annie 17
light tent 20–21

macro shots 16, 20–21
maker faires 24
maker movement 4, 5, 24
modes 16

negatives 11
Niépce, Joseph Nicéphore 8

Pfeil, Jonas 27
photo sharing 4, 15, 24–25, 26
photojournalism 6
pinhole viewer 12–13
point of view 6, 7, 21, 25
Polaroid camera 9
portraits 16, 17, 18, 26

rule of thirds 16, 17

Sasson, Steve 15
scale 6, 25
shutter speed 7, 10
smartphones 5, 15, 18, 22, 23, 24, 28
space exploration 27

trick photography 6, 25
tripods 18, 19, 21